THE SEASONS OF LIFE

"In the light both of the Bible and of modern science . . . we are confronted not with an abstract and generalized man, but with men who are concrete and personal. They are always *in their context,* in a certain relationship to the world, to others, and to God. They are always changing. This changing is made up of seasons, stages in their lives, each of which has its own characteristics and peculiar laws. . . . It is in this life story that God's plan may be accomplished.

"This is what is intimated by the title THE SEASONS OF LIFE: a man in movement, continually undergoing change, a man living a history, unfolding from his birth until his death. The very movement implies meaning in life."

PAUL TOURNIER is a Swiss physician who has made a significant contribution to our understanding of psychiatry and its relation to the Christian faith. Among his books are THE MEANING OF GIFTS, TO UNDERSTAND EACH OTHER, SECRETS, TO RESIST OR TO SURRENDER? Dr. Tournier's writings have been translated into ten languages.

The Seasons of Life

PAUL TOURNIER

Translated by JOHN S. GILMOUR

Pillar Books   New York

A translation of *Les saisons de la vie* by Paul Tournier, published in 1961 by Éditions Labor et Fides, Geneva.

The Scripture quotations in this book are from the Revised Standard Version of the Bible, copyrighted 1946 and 1952 by the Division of Christian Education, National Council of the Churches of Christ in the U.S.A., and used by permission.

THE SEASONS OF LIFE

A PILLAR BOOK
Published by arrangement with John Knox Press

Pillar Books edition published June 1976

ISBN: 0-89129-170-9

Library of Congress Catalog Card Number: 63-8709

Printed in the United States of America

PILLAR BOOKS
(Harcourt Brace Jovanovich)
757 Third Avenue, New York, New York 10017, U.S.A.

The Seasons of Life

I

Our
Life
Seasons

SUCH WAS THE TITLE of a lecture that I was asked to give in Germany last year. When I am asked to prepare such a topic, I like to talk about it with my wife, my patients, and my friends. For it is in dialogue that our thinking is clarified. It is a real service to question others on life's important issues, to invite them to think, to become aware of their personal convictions . . . to express them clearly. Thus it was that I was conversing with a young woman.

"Do you really intend to accept such a topic?" she exclaimed. "It's pure romanticism! First of all, the comparison is false: Seasons in nature continually renew themselves; there's always a springtime to follow the winter. But when we speak of the seasons of life in human existence, we are referring to something quite the opposite: a one-way street that ends in death.

"But even more important," she added, "it just isn't

your conception of men to describe them thus as in a closed and inexorable natural evolution. I know you better than that! Your message is of the miraculous: that man, unlike nature, can have springtimes in autumn."

Yes, there can be springtimes in autumn! This is what distinguishes man. I thought immediately of an old professor who discovered faith at over eighty years of age, and who kept repeating, "I'm but a little child; my life has just begun!" This friend had been raised in a very high moral idealism, but completely void of religion. And then most unexpectedly he met the Lord. Completely overwhelmed, he surrendered to God. His whole life seemed transformed before his very eyes; he was beginning to see it now in its true perspective. Hence his oft-repeated exclamation, "I'm but a little child!"

As a matter of fact, he had become young again, physically as well as emotionally. The grace of God penetrates the whole person. In all the organs, it modifies the body's physiological phenomena, as well as the psychic. Yet his phrase "little child" was somewhat forced. He was still over eighty, and still had to take this fact into account no matter how much he felt the reality of new life. Nor could he erase his past, everything that he'd lived and gathered by experience. His enlightenment had only changed and given a new meaning to his total life experience. God's miracles do not free us from obedience to the natural order which he has established for our life.

This is what Thomas Aquinas expressed in his famous dictum, *gratia non tollit naturam*: Grace does not suppress nature. Indeed not, for man belongs to nature by the will of God, and no spiritual experience, no matter how profound it may be, frees him from his natural state. This is clearly inferred by the story of creation. Man is the object of a special creative act which fundamentally distinguishes him from the animals. However, his creation is part and parcel of the creation-process of all nature. He is the last creation, God's masterpiece. More precisely, it is the woman, whose creation follows that of the man, who is the consummation of nature.

All the Bible shows us man as an integral part of nature. He can arise to conscience and to reason; he can stand apart from the world and see it objectively, study it scientifically, and admire it in faith. But he remains a part of this world. No progress in knowledge nor boldness of faith can set him free from nature. When the psalmist sings his praise of God's handwork in nature, immediately afterward he evokes man as being nature's greatest wonder. And then all of those passages, for example, where Christ compares man to a tree, one who must receive the divine life into him so as to bring forth fruit—all of these underline man's integration in nature.

From this biblical down-to-earth point of view, the divine life-giving sap is not the Holy Spirit only. It is also the life-force, given by God, which determines his physical phenomena; again, it is also the libido which propels his psychic mechanisms. As a part of nature, man is subject to its forces and its laws. But he is distinct from the animal in that God has created him "in his image," that is, a spiritual as well as a natural being. He belongs to two worlds at the same time, the natural and the supernatural, even though he may not yet have become aware of this through faith. This is what confers upon him an eternal mystery. This is what explains how man may appear so self-contradictory, how the best and the worst are inextricably mixed together in him.

Thus, though we can to some extent foresee a man's development according to natural laws, nevertheless there still remains an unpredictable quotient. His development is subject to upheaval by events in his spiritual life. With man there are always surprises, surprises for bad and/or for good. For example, my old professor friend who felt like a child at over eighty. Other examples are Samuel or David, who, though children, showed more maturity than adults. God had spoken to them. Or again, the children whom Jesus pointed out as examples to disciples, and declared riper for the Kingdom of God than the old theologians who understood nothing of his message.

We are therefore constantly exposed to two dangers in the study of man. We may, on the one hand, see nothing more than the natural being, and thus remain blind to the constant reverberation of his spiritual life upon his natural development. On the other hand, like the young woman mentioned earlier, we may see only the spiritual being, and thus ignore the role of his natural life. Thus we see doctors who, in the healing of diseases, perceive only the natural animal in their client. They treat him as if they were veterinarians, quite oblivious of the constant influence of spiritual life upon health. Inversely, we see spiritual healers who condemn any recourse to scientific medicine. They show in this way that they've forgotten that man, as God has made him, is a part of nature, subject to its laws and curable by natural means.

What then makes the study of man so prodigiously interesting and difficult is his belonging to two worlds at the same time: the natural world and the supernatural world. I emphasize *at the same time*. I must insist that our usual distinction between natural and supernatural is artificial, abstract; it is a purely mental division. Man does not have two lives, natural and supernatural: He has only one, his real life. Neither does he have two histories. He has only one, the real one he lives every moment of his existence.

Therefore, it is ever in vain to seek a line of demarcation between nature and spirit. There is no demarcation possible between two realities which are fused together, or which at the least are completely superimposed every step of the way. In the same series of phenomena and events which constitute a man's life, we can read, as naturalists, a simple mechanical unfolding of causes and effects, or else, as G. Gusdorf has said, we can in a "second reading" see a spiritual destiny being played out. The spiritual life is not made up of a few exceptional events, but of the whole of life, to which it gives meaning. Life is meaningless if it is but a blind series of phenomena. We strike the same difficulty when we seek—always in vain—a demarcation between body and soul. Body and soul also are abstract concepts, inventions of our mind. There never is anything other than the man, who is at the same time body and soul.

This double belonging of man to two worlds, to the world of nature and to the world of spirit, remains an impenetrable mystery for us. We find it difficult to understand how, for man, natural phenomena always have a spiritual meaning, and how the supernatural is ever present in the natural. It appears as if these two worlds were inescapably opposed, as if man on this earth lives, as the philosophers have put it, in a perpetual tension between the demands and inexorable laws of his nature and of his spiritual life. Our mind is seeking a concept which can reconcile somehow these two aspects of human life.

I doubt if we can find a more satisfactory one than the biblical concept of the divine plan. From a biblical viewpoint, there is a universal plan of God which gives meaning to world history, and which philosophers and theologians are uncovering. But what concerns us as practitioners is that God's plan is not just general and universal; it is also individual and detailed. There is a divine plan for every man, in which each event of his life has its place. Nature is included in this plan, as well as every inspiration received from God. God leads us both by nature and by his calls; he accomplishes his plan by natural means as well as by those which we call supernatural.

We can see, then, that the conception of a divine plan brings together and harmonizes those elements which we distinguish and set against each other in our abstract thinking: nature and spirit. God reigns over nature: He bends it to his plan. But not just over nature! Not just man's animal life but his total life; God reigns over that which in man goes beyond the natural and animal as well. Hence, what must interest us in studying man is no longer our abstractions—body, soul, nature, spirit—it is rather his real life, concrete and personal, his life history, his continuous breaking into the future. It is in this life story that God's plan may be accomplished. This is what is intimated by the title *The Seasons of Life*: a man in movement, continually undergoing change, a man living a history, unfolding from his birth until his death. The very movement implies meaning in life.

For a long time our approach to the study of man was static. In effect, we ignored both time and space. In order to study man, we stopped the course of his life history in order to pinpoint it at a given moment. We likewise set aside his social and physical environment. What is more, we even isolated each of his organs and each of their functions. It must be admitted that the gains of this analytical method were phenomenal. Nevertheless, what was gained in precision was lost in terms of an over-all view, of an understanding of the human person himself. So much is this so that we have a vast knowledge about man, a storehouse of detailed information, but we lack a definition of what man is. We are beginning to feel that we are losing the meaning of man and that all our detailed knowledge cannot supply the answer.

Yet, for a century now science had tended to rediscover the importance of movement, of becoming. This began with paleontology, which attempted to understand man by the study of his slow prehistoric development. The historical method was introduced in sociology. We try to explain the present in terms of its causes in the past. Just think for a moment of nineteenth-century psychology. It described the "soul's functions" of imagination, will, and reason. It was an abstract and theoretical analysis of a being which does not exist, torn out of the moving current of life. When a man lacked will, he was termed abulic or impulsive, which really explained nothing at all since no one asked what had provoked the appearance of the symptom.

The great merit of Freud was in creating a dynamic psychology: Powerful forces are constantly at work in the human soul and the vicissitudes of their conflicts determine the behavior of the man. Here was rediscovered the sense of living movement, of the link between past, present, and future, of continuous change in man, of the seasons of life. What explains today's man is everything that he has lived up till now plus those needs which are normal for his age.

Until Freud, the child was considered to be an adult in miniature. It is as if we considered springtime to be a miniature summer. Now, however, the child has been shown to have his own psychology, which we must study instead of wanting just to teach the child from an adult viewpoint. This revolution has had far-reaching results. It has remolded all of modern psychology, even that of those thinkers who have opposed Freud. From that time on man has no longer been studied at a given moment of his existence, but throughout his continuous evolution. Scholastic discussions on his "faculties" have lost all their interest; what counts is his lived experience: the events, the decisive happenings of his life, the inner and subjective impressions which he has experienced.

Then came Martin Buber. He emphasized the interpersonal encounter, the human experience *par excellence,* not the encounter with man in general, but with a given man in particular, a "thou" with whom a personal relationship can be established. This too is movement, an event which provokes its inner repercussion. Man is no longer to be studied as an isolated being, but as a part of the social community which ceaselessly is shaping him, and as ceaselessly is itself changing.

Finally today, phenomenological psychology considers man "in his situation." It shows how he integrates himself into his world, projects himself into his work, his play, and into his people, and how he assimilates things into his own being. Thus the current of life has been rediscovered, the element of perpetual becoming in all its infinite complexity. Man today is a history, a personal history.

Thus science has closed the gap with the biblical

viewpoint, for nowhere does the Bible treat man in an abstract or a dogmatic manner. The Bible tells stories of men. It shows men, not man. What counts is that which has happened to such and such a man, at a particular moment of his existence. The Bible shows man in his living, in the midst of conflicts, of passions and forces which determine his behavior; it shows him in his encounter with the other, in that encounter which is personal beyond all others, his meeting with God. Even God himself is not the far-off, infinite, and unmovable god of the philosophers. He is the living God, the acting and the re-acting God who intervenes in history, both in the history of the world and in that of each man.

History means destiny. It is precisely by rediscovering this sense of movement, this sense of the oneness of life in which each event is tied to its past and to its future, that we rediscover also that which is distinctly human and which remained elusive when we isolated man and stopped his "time clock" in order to study him. No moment of life has meaning in and of itself; meaning is found in the series of moments which transforms man step by step and carries him along in his development. Man's destiny is being decided in each event of his life.

Man can change. Here, too, science agrees with the Bible. If psychotherapy heals men, it is because it changes them. It brings into play a new determinism which modifies their development. It tears them from automatic internal compulsions, which are a legacy of their past, so that they can open up to a new freedom. Men in the Bible changed, too; that is the striking feature of their stories. By confronting events, by encountering other men, and by meeting God, their behavior changed. It is from the transformation of their lives that the fulfilling of a destiny becomes evident. They gained a higher degree of freedom, and they found meaning to their lives.

In the light both of the Bible and of modern science, then, we are confronted not with an abstract and generalized man, but with men who are concrete and personal. They are always *in their context,* in a certain relationship to the world, to others, and to God. They are always changing. This changing is made up of seasons, stages in their lives, each of which has its own characteristics and peculiar laws. Periods of crises mark the changes of season: puberty, menopause, the onset of death—this evolution can be more or less normal, or it can be tampered with, speeded up, or slowed down. Thus in our day we see a growing precocity in youth. Our children of fifteen live the experiences which we lived at twenty, and at twenty they show every sign of having reached the age of disillusionment.

II

from Springtime to Summer

IT IS ESPECIALLY this stage—the passing from childhood to adulthood—that has been studied in modern psychology. We shall not mention here all of Freud's theories on the developmental stages of the soul from infancy to adulthood. Let us simply affirm that he has conclusively shown that each stage has its own needs and impulsions which demand that they be "drained dry." That is, they must be satisfied before the appearance of the needs and impulsions of the next stage. What is normal at one stage is no longer normal at the next, and we give the name "infantile inclusions" to those childish survivals which may be found in an adult personality.

In the realm of morality, it is dependence upon parents which characterizes the child. The good is that which meets parental approval, that which earns for the child their smiles and affection. The bad is that which the parents forbid, that which brings the anguish of their scoldings. The sense of guilt in the child is born from fear, fear of losing parental love. The adulthood stage, on the other hand, is marked by moral self-direction, the extent of which depends upon the person's becoming aware of the psychic mechanisms which control him.

The whole Freudian program can be stated as the setting man free from the uncontrolled psychic mechanisms of childhood, in order that he may attain the fullness of adulthood. This is by no means an easy transition. No one ever completely accomplishes it. No person is entirely free of infantile inclusions, not even the most distinguished psychoanalysts! All of us, in some areas which we keep more or less secret, remain children. Thus, we may describe the Freudian ideal as "becoming an adult." This ideal is purely naturalistic. Long before Freud, the Apostle Paul expressed it: "When I was a child, I spoke like a child, I thought like a child, I reasoned like a child; when I became a man, I gave up childish ways."

However, if Paul referred to the divine plan of man's seasons in life, the law of progressive change, he did so in order to give a foretaste of man's ultimate destiny, a fullness far more complete, which lies beyond death, and wherein there will no longer be any lack in "love" and "knowledge."

With Jung, there is a subtler and richer vision of human fullness in his concept of integration. Youth, he says, is absolute. It sees life in black and white, as if there were such a thing as light without shadow. There are but two camps, good and evil, the just and the wicked. Hence, a young person remains hidden to himself, repressing into his unconscious that part of himself which displeases and shames him. This is true of certain of his functions as well as of certain bad impulsions. One day he comes to see that here in this world evil is inextricably mixed up with good, that there is no good man without his faults, nor wicked man without his virtues. He sees that the whole gamut of real humanity is in himself, good and bad, those qualities which he was afraid he lacked as well as those which he tried to disown. He realizes that he can only attain fullness by accepting his own complete nature, including his "shadow."

At this point the young man may balk, he may rebel and repress this unwelcome knowledge; he may become skeptical and disillusioned, he may take the path of regression. Or else, he may take the way of integration, the way of courageous insight. This is the path of unceasing discovery for him, both of hitherto unknown resources in himself and of his inescapable misery. In other words, it is a constant and progressive discovery of life as it really is. Here we see clearly that Jung is treating more than just the narrow transitional phase from child to adult. He is already outlining the change from man's summer to autumn. For, normally, an adult's life is still filled with youth's idealism. In fact, the dynamism of adult action is normally fed by the carry-over of youthful idealism, whereas the key to a successful older life is the wisdom that comes from the way of integration. Let us hasten to add that, with Jung, integration has a spiritual as well as a natural meaning because it is the fruit of an inner urging of the Spirit.

One can see an analogy between the above-described transition and the change which is noticeable in the Bible from the Old to the New Testament. The Old Testament is centered upon the Law. It sets in radical opposition the just and the wicked. It tells men that in order to "obtain life," that is, the fullness of life, they by their own efforts must rigorously obey the Law. Now in the New Testament, it is precisely against those who carried scrupulous obedience to the Law to its ultimate degree, against the Pharisees, that Jesus Christ took his stand. Behind the "outward appearance" of their fine virtues he showed that "within, they are filled . . . with all corruption." As Paul, another Pharisee, would later explain, it is their very attempt to win the righteousness of the Law which is their undoing. Their pretended moral power prevents them from receiving true salvation, which he, Paul, received by grace. That is to say, he received salvation only after having accepted his inability to win it by his own merits.

There is therefore a striking parallel today between the views of science and of faith. Both see man as being drawn through a continuous changing, which, from one step to another, leads him to some destination. This implies meaning to his evolving existence. The same parallel is found when scientists and believers study the factors that favor or hinder this evolution. No longer is it a question of helping men by hit or miss methods; both realize that it is a matter of taking away the hindrances so that the natural development can again take its course. The psychotherapist plays the role of the husbandman in Christ's parable who digs a trench all around the barren fig tree and spreads manure there so that its natural life may revive, bloom forth, and bear fruit.

As an example, we may consider four important factors in development. The first is love. The whole work of the Freudian school has set forth the child's vital need of love, protection, and tender care. Every impediment to love will hinder his natural development

23

and later on may well hold him back from achieving adulthood. We discover many symptoms of the "neurosis of abandonment" throughout the whole human race. For no matter how great the parental love may be, there is always an element that is lacking. The Bible well knows this and shows us this humanity always uneasy, bottled up, hardened, frustrated, the prey of bitter nostalgia for the paradise which has been lost. The answer is the love of God. I know something about this, having been orphaned of both parents and having been healed of the consequences of this loss only after I was seized by the greatness of God's love. The Bible is the proclamation of God's love, a love without limit and without condition. It is more than a proclamation; it is a proof. For, as John states it, the supreme testimony of his love is in having sent his only Son, in having assumed in him all our humanity, in all its suffering and isolation, even unto death. This is an altogether personal love. Thus Jeremiah understood that God had loved him before he was ever born or conceived in the womb of his mother and had called him personally, by name.

A second factor is suffering. Suffering can be a factor in changing a man. Doubtless we have met individuals who seemed to us unable to rise above a certain level of development, and the thought has come to us that only the experience of suffering could lead them any further. There's the case of Suzanne Fouché, that woman whose life has been nothing but sickness, pain, and weakness ever since her sixteenth year. Yet what a tremendous ministry to mankind she has fulfilled! She writes so simply, "What my body loses my spirit can make up. To know suffering . . . is it not to know life itself?" Just lately I saw once again a man who had come to see me the day after a terrifying experience.

24

He had before his very eyes witnessed the accidental death of his son. The other day he told me that his son's death had brought him into the Kingdom of God.

We doctors know well that suffering can have the very opposite effect; it can be a terrible obstacle to the unfolding of a man's life. It can become a meeting point with other men and with God, but it can also be felt as an insurmountable barrier of isolation. Thus Kierkegaard wrote, "My life is one great suffering, unknown and incomprehensible to all others." Suffering, then, has no great value in and of itself. This is why Suzanne Fouché does not speak of suffering only, but of the "knowledge of suffering," that is to say, of the way in which we live our suffering.

The Bible expresses it on every page. It presents abundantly and with realism every form of human suffering, moral and physical, together with its liberating or its destroying consequences, depending upon whether it meets the response of surrender or of rebellion. Think for a moment of the people of Israel, wandering for forty years in the wilderness. The Bible shows God always compassionate in the face of human suffering: Jesus Christ healing the sick, restoring the outcasts, sending forth those who have given themselves to him so that they may help their brothers in suffering.

Then there is the factor of identification. It plays an important part in human development. By imitation the child begins to speak. By identification with her mother the little girl plays with her doll and comes to long for the day when she will have children of her own. By identification with his father the boy one day casts off his childish games. He turns to more manly attractions. He starts smoking secretly, in order to prove to himself that he is a man. He begins to work, no longer out of obedience, but in order to make for himself a career in the world. By identification with their elders a boy and a girl develop their first love relationships.

The other day one of my patients, now in middle-life, told me that she identifies with the artless maidens in the motion pictures at their first awakenings to love. Of course she felt that this "backward identification" was abnormal. Nevertheless, it seems to me to be a sign of growth, for this woman has been blocked in this area of her life ever since childhood. She simply has to go through the stages which she never went through at the proper time, if she is to grow beyond them.

However, if the identification of a boy with his father stimulates his development, it also limits it to the dimensions of his father. His father has his failings and his prejudices. If the son remains a prisoner of his model, he will never attain his own true stature. He will need to identify with heroes of legend and history: an explorer, a scientist, an artist, a saint. Even so, every identification but one has its limitations. One day I heard my colleague from Florence, Dr. Assagioli, develop this point before the Philosophical Society of Geneva. He spoke on identification with Christ, just as Paul also expressed it: "It is no longer I who live, but Christ who lives in me."

Finally, there is adaptation. Goethe wrote, "To live is to adapt." This is the concept of growth *par excellence*. The psychologist sees every blockage in life as a sign of failure in adaptation. Each new situation demands, especially of the child, but also throughout the whole of life, a "going beyond" of himself and of his habits which is far from easy. If he succeeds in this, he grows by this victory. If the effort is beyond his capacity, he regresses. There are parents who in their solicitude for their child try to spare him every effort. They overprotect him from the hazards of life. They keep him a child and hold back his growth. In this way they prepare him for what later will be a total impossibility—his adaptation to life. Others, on the other hand, in their desire to make a man of their child, expose him too early to efforts of adaptation that are too great for him. They make him grow old prematurely, and because he never fully was a child, he will never fully become an adult.

We are all aware of dangers in a too complete adaptability. Everyone has known couples who tell us with frankness and pride that they've never quarreled. Yet, they seem so colorless. It is obvious that their *bonne entente* is due to one of the partners having lost all his own personality by a complete adaptation to the other. Such couples' lives are dull, stagnant, ingrown, incapable of adaptation to the larger community life around them. The husband who has broken his wife's own personality and has enslaved her to himself, no longer can put up with his friends' contradictions. He locks himself up in his own solitude.

When God said, "It is not good that man should be alone," he intended, by giving him a partner quite different from himself, to force him to face up to a difficult process of mutual adaptation. He intended him to go beyond himself instead of avoiding the conflict by surrendering to his wife or by enslaving his wife. In other words, he needs to grow up.

Likewise, we all know of Christians who say that they have never doubted. Their lives seem so pale, so far off from the heroic adventure that is faith. The most fruitful believers tell us shamedly of the inner battles that have torn them between doubt and faith. And the great Bible characters from Abraham or Moses right through Jacob, Jeremiah, Peter, and Paul all show us their conflict-filled lives, their revolts against heaven, their refusals to adapt to a God who was too demanding of them. They show us as well their reconciliation to that God. God loves those who don't give in without a fight!

It is by their very battles that those men grew. Jacob, on the morning after his dramatic nightlong wrestle with God, awoke hardly able to stand up. But he woke up a changed man. He had entered into a new season in life. The same was true of Abraham after his importunate prayers that Sodom be spared from the wrath of God, of Moses after his obstinate debate with the Lord before the burning bush, of Jeremiah the timid after all his refusals to bear a message of destruction, of Peter after his denial, of Paul after the road to Damascus. The same was true of all the other biblical heroes. They were real men! They knew how to defend themselves; they would not give in easily. Therefore their surrender had nothing in it that resembled childish dependency. Their very surrender was an act of manly courage. It brought them to human fulfillment and opened up human history to new seasons of life.

III

Christianity:
Freedom
or Bondage

HOW IS IT, then, that in our churches there are so many souls that seem crushed down or even childish? A Roman Catholic colleague from abroad came to see me one day and told me that he wanted to organize a colloquy of theologians and medical doctors to discuss the question of "growing into adulthood." He told me that it was because he, with some friends, had become quite disturbed about the great number of religious persons who are childish and stunted, and the small number of developed personalities. "I rather believe the situation is different among Protestants," he added. How I hated to disillusion him! Our Protestant churches are likewise filled, for the major part, with sad, broken, and snuffed-out personalities. We may even find a greater proportion of neurotics than in Catholic lands or among those who have lost contact with the church.

Psychotherapists have remarked on this, and it is not

surprising that many of them accuse the churches of choking off the unfolding of personality instead of exalting it. Some go so far as to pose as apostles of a new gospel that is able to set religious people free from the anguish and the inhibitions which paralyze them and hold them back in a prolonged childhood, only to precipitate them into a premature senility. Doubtless this reflection came to our minds when a few moments ago I made reference to a complete agreement between psychologists and the churches, agreement with regard to human fulfillment. But now it would appear, to some at least, that psychologists were working for mature men whereas the churches were trying to break men. Where does such a conclusion find any grounds?

It comes from a perversion of Christianity. I am convinced that the criticism of the psychologists cannot touch sane and authentic Christianity. But it does touch the *moralism* so prevalent in our churches today. In place of the great liberating experience of divine grace, our moralism substitutes the obsessive fear of committing a mistake. Dr. Théo Bovet of Basle has told us the story of the pastor who asked his young people in the catechism class, "What is religion?" A boy immediately replied, "Religion shows us the things we must not do." Nor can we pretend to be surprised by such an answer. For most of our people today to be religious means to make a continuous effort to be *good* (like a little child) and to keep oneself from everything forbidden.

How very far we are from the Bible! Let's re-examine the great men of the Bible. What do you find? Assassins, liars, jealousy-blinded characters, traitors, puffed-up snobs, adulterers, rebels, and prostitutes. Don't get me wrong; I'm not advocating sin; what I am trying to say is that the religion which the Bible presents is not a moralistic system. Religion therein means

31

to seek God and his grace with utter passion. Moralism is simply seeking oneself, that is, pretending to be able to know both good and evil. It means eschewing every occasion of error, by virtue of scruple and self-repression. Taken to its logical end, it simply means that we do not need either God or his grace.

We can recognize in this fear of making an error the very legalistic and childish mentality of which we have spoken above. Moralism, in fact, constitutes an infantile regression within the churches. But let a wave of persecution come over the church and, lo, she once again rises to heroism! She once again is set alive by virile men, indefatigable warriors who lay ahold of God and will not let him go, who seize his Word, who are turned inside out by his Spirit, who are overwhelmed by his love. They live in the reality of God, and from him they receive an unchangeable faithfulness. All the rationale of moralism is swept away in an instant. On the other hand, when the church is recognized by the world, she withdraws into a meticulous moralism wherein there is no room for the adventure of faith. How tragic, how pitiable it is to see a good and religious man find no other way of rediscovering the thrill of living than by falling one day into some stupid adultery—"He who would be an angel becomes a beast," said Blaise Pascal.

But, someone will object, what do you make of the demand of Christ that we deny ourselves? Is that not sufficient reason for the Christian's not being able to adhere to the psychologists' ideal of human fulfillment? Is not their plea for self-affirmation radically excluded by the death to self which Paul calls for? Here we are faced with a tragic misunderstanding. I find this as much among church people as among their adversaries. Show me someone, anyone, who better affirmed himself than the Apostle Paul! The self-denial required by the gospel is not at all a withdrawal into a truncated life of perpetual childhood. Self-denial is the renunciation of a self-directed life, for the very purpose of attaining a far greater fullness under the direction of God.

Here again we come back to the concept of the plan of God. God wills our development, our fulfillment; he has written it into the law of nature. Yet, his plan aims at a far greater fullness than that which naturalists can imagine. This is a fullness which cannot be attained by nature alone, no matter how harmonious it may be; this fullness comes to those who are directed by God, those who have surrendered themselves to him. In every passage wherein Jesus speaks of self-denial there is a promise which follows, a promise of riches "an hundredfold." Even when he calls us to "lose" our life, he adds that it is in order to save it. It is in order that we may find the real life, the life which is far more fruitful.

Therefore we are faced with the question of life's fulfillment. It is the law of the greater fulfillment which Christ has given us. Life with God is the greatest adventure imaginable. The "new birth" of which he spoke to Nicodemus—a man who had reached the peak of natural honors—this new birth includes the Freudian concept of "becoming adult" and the Jungian concept of "integration." Yet, it means far more than these. Jesus said it himself: It is the Kingdom of God; it is eternal life. It is, in other words, the opening up to an entirely new season, a season which contains the principle of an eternal fullness, freed from the inexorable limit set by death, referred to by the young woman mentioned at the beginning of this book.

But let's not anticipate the autumn. The law of childhood is that of passive submission, of concern for the forbidden: It is the age of legalism. But this concern cannot remain dominant through our whole life without bringing with it infantile regression. Christ himself has stated the law of summer: that ye shall bear fruit. What God expects from the life of a mature man is that he should bear fruit. This image of the fruit-laden tree is the symbol of development. Jesus added to this, "If you abide in me, so shall you bear much fruit."

The meaning then of the revolution in our life that comes through surrender to Christ is not at all that of limitations set upon us. It is, on the contrary, the enlarging of our life. Recently I attended a reunion banquet with my old friends, fellow students back in college. I had the feeling of being among the youngest of them. Imagine, I who have gone through several crises and upsets, I who had thought that the whole direction of my life had been changed, I discovered an amazing consistency and faithfulness to my earliest hopes and aspirations. Yet, many of those present who have apparently gone on steadily in their chosen vocations have lost this or have lost much of their career's "first love."

Thus the law of summer must be action. It is the establishment of a home and career and their continued development. For the married woman priority belongs to the home while for the man the career comes first. Nevertheless, neither the man nor his wife can achieve fulfillment unless their action embraces both home and career. The wife must identify herself with her husband's work, and the husband must not allow his career so to capture him that he neglects his role in the home. I shall never forget one man at the very height of success and recognition. He came to see me once and said, "I have wrecked my life, for I have been a complete success in business, but I've let my marriage go on the rocks."

The number of such men who come to my office and repeat those same words simply amazes me, men who are trying to make an honest appraisal of their lives. "I've wrecked my life!" Of course, they are guilty of exaggeration. I could protest and point out to them all those elements of real worth that they have achieved in life. But it would be so many words in vain. You cannot help men by arguing with them; you can help them by understanding them. So I maintain silence so as not to interrupt this painful and all-important self-examination.

Their blurted-out words are a cry of alarm, which expresses something deeply written into the heart of every man. Life is not a harmless diversion or a chance adventure; it is the crucial game which we can play only once. This game must of necessity end in victory or defeat. Oh, we can alibi all we want on our strokes of good or ill fortune, but the final result is that which counts. Everybody shares the feeling that life is an all-important gamble. We may differ as to our criteria of what constitutes success, but the necessity to succeed is universal.

IV
Fulfillment

TO SUCCEED! Take a look at this couple as they stand before their baby's cradle. Already they are gripped by the thought of the unknown future of their little one. Will he succeed in life? Perhaps it is then that they realize that the concern for success has never left them for a moment, that it has been the driving force in their work, the motivation behind the good appearance they put up and the polished phrases they pronounce, in order to bring out the best in their capabilities. They live ceaselessly under the impression, consciously or otherwise, that they stand before an invisible jury which is going to pronounce its verdict: success or failure.

Why are they going to teach good manners to this little child? Why good conduct in society, why morals, why such angry insistence if he resists? Why will they push him in his studies, in spite of resistance, why will

38

they be careful about his friendships, why will they be anxious over his choice of fiancée? Why? So that he will succeed in life. Even his religious training can be considered as giving him a little more chance. Thus unbelieving parents scold their child for having missed a session of catechism and point out to him that it could always be handy later on in life.

Again, let us consider the industrialist who overworks to the point of a heart attack, who complains of never having a moment for leisure. Why does he lay so much work upon himself? To earn money?—Not at all! He is prisoner of his success; if a business does not continue to grow it is considered to be failing. When he buys a high-priced car, it isn't so much for comfort or for vacation trips—for which in any case he no longer finds time—as for a symbol of success. There are even those who have taken a mistress simply for this reason.

Don't smile; no one eludes this mechanism. The objective may differ, but no one is insensitive to success. It is the joy of success which leads the scientist or technician from discovery to discovery. A problem faces him: He has no repose until he has solved it. Thus those fine people who, because of the atomic bomb, propose the limitation of scientific research are hoping for an Utopian world. There is no preacher who is insensitive to the crowd which comes to hear him at church, nor to any humble soul who compliments him afterward. Even as I write, I want very much to succeed in this book. He who loses the hope of success falls into depression. Or else he looks for another way in which to succeed.

All this contains, then, a profound and universal truth about men. It is our intuition that there is a life plan for everyone, and that its accomplishment will mean life's fulfillment. Each of us likewise feels that fulfillment is much more than just what we commonly understand by the phrase "success in life." Success in life is the subject matter of many "how-to" books, especially in America. They are often full of good common sense, wise and useful advice. Yet such success strikes one as hardly more than external and socially evaluated; it doesn't reach down to the inner being. This was evident in the man mentioned earlier who, though he had nothing for which he could envy any other person as far as success is concerned, nevertheless declared that he had ruined his life.

There is no use in trying to console him, in telling him that he is too ambitious, that he should be content with what he has. All of us feel that there are certain things which we value so highly that their absence cannot be made up for by any other gain, no matter how brilliant. Every other prize would be but poor consolation, incapable of long deluding us. The day that a man realizes this fact, he may enter a terrible crisis in life. His gains all of a sudden strike him as void of any value whatsoever, and he is in danger of sinking into a bitter and cynical disillusionment.

Thus do we meet both men and women, at the very peak of their productive life and given to many worthy activities, who cannot forgive themselves for having neglected, in the whirl of their absorbing activities, some inner call. The call felt in youth they left unanswered. Again, though we can succeed in life by attainment in any one area, no one feels that he can fulfill his life in just any sphere. Such fulfillment implies a choice, a scale of values, the idea not just of any plan one might draw up at will, or by guess, more or less as he goes along, but of a quite personal plan.

It is the idea of God's plan which every man bears in his soul, even if he is an unbeliever. In this case, he will

40

be careful not to call it God's plan. But the concept remains the same, like the plan of God: An apple tree will bear apples and not pears. It is the idea that life is a gift which implies responsibility, that God—be he known or unknown—expects something very definite of us, and not just anything. This God, as nature has shown, loves diversity: He has created millions of species of plants and animals, every one different from the next, and what prodigious diversity he has shown in creating men! Therefore, because for him no life is just one more, each has received his own characteristics and particular talents.

To this first diversity of inborn gifts and hereditary tendencies is added the second, that of life's events which contribute toward fashioning our personality and tracing our pathway, and again the third, that of the inner leadings which sometimes grip our mind and bring us to see a goal and meaning to our life, a direction to take, a vocation. Every man feels this. No one feels that he must proceed by mere chance or walk in the steps of another. Rather he feels that he is on a quite unique pathway which must lead him to some destination still unknown to him. He has been feeling his way along in a continual mixture of darkness pierced by rays of light, through acts of obedience and through many errors: It is only afterward that the events of his personal life show meaning.

It seems that an invisible hand is guiding him toward a goal of which he was unaware before, and, I would emphasize, guiding him even through his mistakes. Here is a great mystery. The Bible is very eloquent on this point. Reread it, and you will see it on every page: God's plan is fulfilled not just through the obedience of inspired men, but also through their errors, yes, their sins. It culminates in the case of Judas, who symbolizes all human sin, and yet who has his place in the divine plan of redemption. Jesus himself said to him, "What you are going to do, do quickly." I say this in order to reassure many who have despaired to the point of believing that their life is henceforth lost because at some given moment an error in judgment has misdirected their course. None can step outside God's plan. At every moment, no .matter what the accumulated ruins may be, there is a plan of God to be found.

At every moment the given elements of the past, the mistakes as well as the talents, can take on new meaning by a divine illumination. Here we rediscover the intimate meeting of natural and supernatural of which we have already spoken. Take for example a man like Saint Paul, with a temperament supercharged with aggressiveness. He put his whole, implacable, relentless, and absolute nature into persecuting the early church. Then he met Christ on the road to Damascus, and the whole course of his life was changed. Notwithstanding, his natural character was not changed. We still find his aggressiveness, which in the hand of God becomes a mighty instrument in the spread of the gospel.

You see how far we are from moralism. It is no longer a question of knowing whether our character is good or bad, but whether or not we are using it according to the plan of God. This plan includes periods of delay. It isn't just a matter of doing what God wants, but of doing it *when* he wants. Dr. Bovet of Basle has insisted upon this biblical concept of God's moment, the καιρός , in his little book *L'art de trouver du temps (The Art of Finding Time)*. Often in the Bible these expressions reappear: "the hour was not yet come . . ." and "when the time had fully come . . ." Often Jesus spoke of the delays in nature, of the farmer's patience who has to wait for the harvest. There are times of necessary ripening.

Ripening is essential to the very quality of the fruit. Hence the summer season of our active adulthood must not be made up of activity only. Meditation is needed. And throughout the season's progress such meditation must take up more and more place. For it is therein that takes place the seeking of God's plan, of a personal scale of values. It is the arena of decision, in order that our action may not be simply agitation and the spreading out of self but become a lifework. It is not good that this decision be taken too early in the season. It does not seem auspicious that young men try prematurely to choose their philosophy of life, their goal, their faith, their wife. For the very value of the choice, it is important that first they have faced a diversity of ideas, concepts, and environments.

Yet the further the season advances, the greater becomes the need to choose. To live is to choose. Those who through a childish notion of what fullness implies want to lose none of their human inheritance, sacrifice nothing, give up nothing, lose out in spreading themselves too thin. They never attain true fullness. The example of André Gide, so sincere in this way, together with his confessions in the eventide of life, is most impressive. It is rather a case of youth which is unable to go beyond a certain point in order to attain the fulfillment of age. The further one advances, the more such a conception of fullness appears Utopian. Fullness cannot be an accumulation of successes and activities in every possible human domain.

When we are young it is still possible to fool ourselves by charging to the future what the present still lacks. Sooner or later, however, we have to wake up. Behind every objective we attain there gradually take shape ten others. Far from the gradual filling in of what life lacks, this appears ever to expand. We have to renounce far more than we accomplish. If there are satisfactions, there are also disillusionments; if there are successes, there are necessarily failures as well. The day comes when we understand that the latter have been more fruitful perhaps than the successes. For it is they which force us to revise our system of values, our soon-to-follow law of old age.

Sickness can suddenly overtake us at the very height of career and in the full frenzy of activity, with the same blow breaking it and, in some ways, revealing its emptiness. Then it is that a man needs to find someone with whom he can talk about the problems beseiging his mind. It will no longer suffice to promise, and do everything to ensure, prompt healing, or even to allow him the hope of taking up again his former rhythm of life. Every sickness heralds the death which one day will come to put an end to our so fragile success. With such sickness, or some other serious setback, old age has begun. Then it is that we realize how inevitably incomplete our life is.

V

from
Summer
to Fall

WHEN DOES old age set in? Somewhere Jung referred to a dream of one of his patients. He explains, for
the reader's understanding, that the patient was forty
years old, the age when life's evening begins to fall,
when after a long upward journey, we must learn to go
back downhill. Jung's intention was certainly not to
pinpoint the date of this change, but to underscore the
necessity of adjusting to it. The change itself may be-
gin quite early: the day, for example, when a woman
admits to herself that her chances of marrying are
rapidly disappearing. Or the day a man realizes that
he has taken the wrong road. Gifted artistically, under
the pressure of his family and for security he took on
an office career. Now he is bored and feels guilty, but
it is too late to undertake a career in art.

It is indeed difficult to help men to see clearly at this
point: Which choice must they resolutely reject? Or

what courageous about-face is demanded of them in order that they may yet fulfill unrealized hopes? Should they risk everything they have in order to try to achieve certain very much desired goals? Or, again, is it foolishness to gamble life's present achievement against the possibility of a particular success, which just the same may not have any definite value? One may long hesitate between the alternatives.

Basically it is a struggle between two concepts of fulfillment: that of summer and that of autumn. Meanwhile, life goes on. A day will come when this woman will know that she definitely never will be able to have children, or that man that he will never gain the chair in philosophy for which he has been preparing since youth. Autumn has arrived.

We cannot recover time. This is clearly seen with those who through sickness have been laid aside from active life for years. If upon their being healed they do not accept their age, but wish to relive the lost years, their lives are thrown out-of-step. They do not win back the past and they lose out in the present. The same thing is true every time failure is not accepted. It is purely a question of age. It is just as unfortunate for a young man to hold the joys and ambitions of his age in skeptical contempt, under pretext that they are short-lived and hardly worthwhile in view of eternity, as it is for another about to enter old age who clings to an unrealized hope as if his life success were absolutely tied to one particular event, valuable though it may be, as if all else were but vain endeavor.

In the Gospels as well, we see both the season of success and the season of setback. Jesus lived both of them, to their fullest, and without reserve. First there were the resounding successes in Galilee which aroused the hopes of growing crowds flocking about him, and which he did not reject, until their intention of making him an earthly king set them in opposition to the plan of God. But there was also the forsaken Christ in his Passion, having suffered setback not only with the people but with his own disciples as well: abandonment and betrayal. "My God! My God! Why hast thou forsaken me?"

Successes have their meaning and there is no question of undervaluing them. However, failures also have their meaning, perhaps a deeper meaning. What gives them all meaning is that they work together toward the fulfillment of God's plan.

What is perhaps more striking is the danger present in certain successes. In history we see this when so many men and nations have marched from victory to victory right on to catastrophe. On the other hand, as Mr. Joseph Folliet says jokingly about England, "She has always quietly gone from defeat to defeat until meeting final victory." We need to realize the dangers of security. I have just returned from Finland. It is from contact with countries like this that I see what menaces my own Switzerland: prosperity and security.

Even in Finland many men told me how nostalgically they look back to the time of the terrible "winter war," in which, against the enemy's hundred-to-one odds, they fought as one man, heroically and extraordinarily.

Prosperity brings a kind of old age, not only premature, but false. It is not the fruit of inner growth or of the careful development of a system of values, but of deadening boredom, the drying up of life itself. Thus we see men literally cave in the moment they achieve the goal which they had set for themselves. One public official throughout his whole career longed to get to the top rung, to become head of the department. His climb took far longer than what he had dreamed. Yet, the day following his long-awaited nomination he fell sick, and he definitely felt that the sickness was not accidental.

Another man fought a certain case in court for years. His whole life aim was to obtain justice. But God knows how many surprises and delays that legal procedure can come up with! Finally, when he won his case, he did not at all experience the sweet taste of victory which he had expected. He is as in a great emptiness, with no strength, nor goal, nor interest in anything. He seems to have lost any purpose in life. The fight for his case had so swallowed him up that it became his whole life goal. And this he lost by his victory. Will he be able to carry through a revision of his value-system, and in time? Will he yet find energy enough to rethink life's meaning, instead of forever rehashing the various episodes of the court case? This is not sure.

Thus, the hour for revision of values necessarily comes for whoever does not die prematurely. Few men successfully meet it. Most men sink into bitterness. They long for the summer of life, now over. They rebel at being disillusioned. Or else they turn to telling over and over again their moments of glory. Self-satisfaction or else rancor: These are but two ways of ruining one's old age. Everyone senses that life fulfillment cannot be compounded of happy adulthood followed by a wrecked old age. Jung said that it is impossible to live the evening of life in the same manner as the morning.

Professor Karlfried von Dürckheim recently told of a visit he had from an old man. The latter was radiant and told with pride how he'd just succeeded in climbing a mountain that younger men would already give up hope of ever attempting. "To me it seems very foolhardy," Dürckheim said quite strongly. To his protesting visitor he further explained, "What use is it to try to prolong, for a very little while and against all the laws of nature, the performance of certain feats which you know you must finally give up?" If the joy of living is tied up in such possibilities, then it is condemned in advance to a rapidly approaching despair.

Yes, this is but another way in which we can refuse to change. True happiness is always linked with deep, inner harmony. It therefore always implies acceptance of one's age: the acceptance of no longer being a child when one has reached the age of adulthood and the giving up of the goals of active life when one is advanced in years. This is the age of retirement, which for some men can be a magnificent experience, while for others it is a cruel trial. Why such differences? Partly, undoubtedly, this comes from differences in temperament. Yet, more so from something else. Those who complain about their retirement are usually the same ones as those who used to complain about their work and longed to be set free from it! Thus the problem is of the soul's condition, of true maturity. The serious question remains to be answered: What is the meaning of life?

We have attempted, in this study of man, to see him as on-the-go, in continual change, like nature itself going from season to season. The question irrepressibly arises: Is this evolving blind? Is it like a chance and purposeless bit of machinery which is self-operating but without any final result? Or, on the other hand, does this pattern of change lead somewhere, and thus confer meaning upon the whole of life? During the summer of life, this question can hardly be entertained.

The goal at that time is the completion of each action undertaken, a goal imposed by nature itself, by the springing forth of desire, ambition, and instinct.

VI

The
Meaning
of Life

THE FURTHER on we go, the more we see time as a diminishing capital. Moreover, its running out goes on at an ever-quickening pace, by virtue of the physiological mechanism described by Carrel. The older one becomes, the shorter the years ahead seem to be, even though there remain yet twenty years, such a long, long time in the eyes of a child. And this takes place just at the time when our strength is diminishing, the time when we must gradually give up doing many things which, a little while before, we did with such ease. I don't think it is accidental that this topic was given to me to develop, for in fact I have just entered my sixties. Already I feel my capacity for work diminishing. Even though I may yet be helpful to a few patients or even write a few more books, all of that will not make much difference now to the sum of my life.

The die is cast. That which I have been able to do,

to learn, or to acquire is gradually losing its value. The *doing* and the *having* are giving way to the *being*. What is important for the aged is not what they are still able to do, nor yet what they have accumulated and cannot take with them. It is what they are. This is the cause of the dreadful feeling of uselessness that so deeply bothers most elderly people. All those concepts of our modern Western civilization, in which effective action is held above all, contribute to their plight. The Greeks of antiquity honored their elders far more than we. Just think of Nestor, their personification of wisdom. For the Greeks, action was above all else a means of acquiring wisdom.

To be fair, we must recognize that the proportion of elderly people was far smaller among the Greeks, and it was much easier to honor them because of their relative scarcity. Nevertheless, ought not our modern world revise its criteria? At least enough to admit that if *doing* is the criterium of summer, something different is needed to measure the autumn? If progress in medicine tends to make our society more and more made up of older people, then a radical and authentic reevaluation of old age is absolutely essential. Yet, is it not the older person himself who must discover this secret, instead of considering himself a worn-out adult?

I say an authentic re-evaluation, for we all know that it is not enough to invent some new life goal by hit-or-miss, some consolation prize for old age. It is the true meaning of life that needs to be discovered. The search for this will be the law of old age, just as assiduous study under authority is that of childhood, and self-directing activity is that of adulthood. I have always very much liked old folk and taken great pleasure in treating them. Doubtless this is because I have felt that it is with them, with the drawing near of death and the new scale of values that this gives, that true values are sifted out, the enduring ones. If living means choosing, and if in adulthood this is true to an ever greater degree, then choosing becomes the supreme vocation of old age, when life has become privation and earthly treasures have lost their glitter.

Then it is that a purely technical and scientific medical care, less and less effective, gives way to an ever more pressing care of the person. The elderly suffer from a great many ills for which not much can be done, unless we are blindly to administer more and more vitamins and hormones. Yet, I do not want to exaggerate. I am not minimizing the devotion applied by the oculist in order to prolong for a time the patient's ability to read. I don't want to scorn his joy at success in so doing. Nor that of the specialist in ears, nose, and throat in prolonging for a time the patient's ability to hear. But the day will come when this ability to read or to hear will depend less on the state of the organs themselves than on the person's inner disposition.

Moreover, if medicine has no other hope to offer than a limited and temporary renewal of a vanishing ability, then it becomes most disillusioning. A few somersaults well on in the autumn of life: These no longer really constitute enjoyment. They strike us more as a break in harmony, and underline the prospect of the more bitter morrow. Sorry figures those retired businessmen who persist in going daily to the office— in order to fool themselves! Everyone around must religiously keep up the act in order to make them believe they are still needed, and at the same time, must carry on the business behind their backs.

Who fails to see that actually they are losing out in the very thing they have, old age itself? To cling to the past, to seek most doggedly to prolong one's time of action means precisely this: living a useless old age. For it is not being consecrated to what it should. If technical medical care has to recede, the doctor's role is now precisely that of making the new transition sure, of preventing a regression. Our task is to help men right to the end, to help them to grow up, and to help them to grow old. The new transition means to face, rather than avoid, this question of the true meaning of life. During their time of action, men found *too easy* answers which now no longer stand up. It means looking ahead instead of behind; it means being set free from the past. Just as it was necessary for the child to free himself of his childish ways in order to achieve adulthood and for the young man to leave his parents in order to marry, even so in order to continue growing, in order to live a meaningful autumn, the old man must free himself from the thought-patterns of adulthood.

There is no question here of scorning the past. Rather, it means profiting from its lesson, a lesson still valid and one whose worth will grow in proportion as the past is left behind. This is the hour when a man looks at his life and seeks to decipher the enigma of its worth. This is the hour when he can do so in serenity, far more than in the midst of adulthood's warfare. This is what we see in all those who come to tell us their life story. Every account of one's life is deformed, unbalanced by conscious or unconscious value-judgments. No one can retell all that he has lived through. We should need more time to tell it than what it took to live through it. Even so, it would never be safe from being deformed to some extent. How hard it is to see with clarity in the overabundance of lived experience!

It is precisely this inability to grasp the whole that forces us to choose. As G. Gusdorf has shown, all in our life is not of equal value. He who would scrupulously record everything in his personal diary may accumulate volumes without gaining any self-understanding. So, the riches of life no longer appear as an endless accumulation like a collection of postage stamps, no matter how well classified. Rather, they lie in those decisive moments when one's life was turned in a new direction. In every life there are a few special moments that count for more than all the rest because they meant the taking of a stand, a self-commitment, a decisive choice. It is commitment that creates the person. It is by commitment that man reveals his humanity.

These turning points in life are generally few in number. They may have been slow, almost unconscious, gradually brought to fruition through extended crises, or they may have been like the flash of lightning, a sudden burst into consciousness of a process worked through in the subconscious. Yet, when we try to understand their essential character, we perceive that they are always an encounter: encounter with an idea or encounter with a person, before which the subject cannot remain neutral. He simply had to take sides, to shoulder responsibility, to commit himself.

It may be the encounter with the woman whose presence will change the whole course of life, because the complete frankness that love implies will force the man to explain his real self to himself, without reserve. Or the encounter with a friend, just one word that he said but the clarity of which will never be lost. Encounter with a book, a film, a fact of nature, a philosopher, or a preacher—suddenly the whole gamble of life is embodied in a particular encounter, which confers on life its whole meaning and all its creative power.

This is because back of every such encounter,

whether we know it or not, there is always an encounter with God, which may be quite transparently evident. Yes, even the moment when a man finds his gospel in Communism and dedicates himself henceforth, body and soul, to it. I am here going beyond all questions of doctrine and of those commitments which lead to the warfare between committed men. I am attempting to grasp the specifically human experience. It is the pressing need to find meaning for one's life, to subordinate the whole of life to that meaning. It is this need, this inner aspiration, which is from God. All the ideologies, doctrines, and formulas drawn up by men will pass; every ideal, too, grows old in turn. Only the true and living God remains.

Thus the knowing encounter with the living God is the greatest possible human event: the human experience *par excellence*. The circumstances and forms of this encounter may be infinitely variating. It always comes as such a surprise that the conviction is inescapable that it is the doing of God, the result of his direct initiative.

A few days ago it was Good Friday. I received, as in every preceding year, a letter from a patient in memory of a certain Good Friday when, though she was all alone in her room, and nothing particular had seemed to lead up to this, all of a sudden she felt the overwhelming presence of God. I had been treating her, without much success, for several years.

Here is a letter from a woman unknown to me. She writes from America. Just before leaving Europe and without knowing why, she slipped one of my books into her suitcase. Aboard the plane, she began turning through a few pages, hit-or-miss. It is because of this that she writes me so kindly. Yet she is under no more illusion than I; my book had no hand in that which took place in her, high above the Atlantic. She says that for years she had been continually asking the same question of every learned person she met, "Who is God?" and that she never received any satisfactory answer. Certainly my book did not give any such reply, either. Never have I pretended to tell who God is!

Here we are on a terrain beyond all the discussions and debates of ideas, yet within the domain of the person. It is the personal presence of God, revealed so suddenly in the plane to that woman. So she writes that it is a new woman who put her foot on America's soil, and one who will never again need to ask another the question, "Who is God?"

As far as theological or philosophical discussion is concerned, such research would belong to the adult age of action. However, no matter at what age this event takes place, the personal encounter with God constitutes the one great fact of existence. It is the only one which throws clear, though somewhat veiled, light upon life's meaning. The encounter may take place in childhood, as with Samuel, or in full manhood and in the midst of professional activity, as with Peter. Again, it may happen in old age, as with Simeon. It always constitutes the sole decisive experience. With Simeon, the older person can say, "Lord, now lettest thou thy servant depart in peace . . . for mine eyes have seen thy salvation." To know God, his grace, his salvation—this is the meaning of life. "What is man's chief end?" wrote Calvin at the outset of his catechism. "To know God. What is his joy? The very same."

You can see that here the limits of the seasons are no longer distinguishable. It is the whole of life that we embrace in one look and that already is overflowing into resurrection. One can come to know God through the docile learning of childhood, in the midst of the full activity of maturity, or in the contemplative age of retirement. It is this *knowing* which remains as the common denominator of all life's stages.

In my childhood I had already come to know God, quite naïvely of course; nevertheless, I thank God for those who led me to him. Yet, it took a revolutionary experience in order for this knowledge to go beyond the abstract nature of a few ideas about God, however right those ideas might have been. I had to meet him in the full activity of adulthood, through dialogue with inspired men. They put my real life, my home and my medical work, under the light of God. Ever since, Jesus Christ has become my unseen companion of every day, the witness of all my successes and all my failures, the confidant of my rejoicings and my times of sadness. It is in this life shared with him that the knowledge of God is continuously strengthened and sharpened. All that I can hope, when my time for action will be over, is that I may yet go further in the riches of this knowledge.

Doubtless, the abundance of life is not attained here below. Yet, it begins here. As Saint Paul wrote, ". . . now we see in a mirror dimly." With him, I know that beyond the winter of death I shall see God face to face, and understand fully, even as I have been fully understood, from before my birth. Thus, without forcing the simile too much, we can compare the time of approaching death with the changing of autumn into winter. And we who are doctors, we who are the first to receive man into this world at his birth, we have the great privilege of faithfully accompanying him right to his last drawn breath, to the very gates of death. We have the great privilege of knowing that all this pathway has meaning, that its destination lies in that mysterious fullness which has been declared unto us.